My China

Poetry written in and about
China, and afterwards...

by

David Lewis Paget

BARR BOOKS

For my Chinese Students
And Friends…

Other Poetry available by the author:

Pen & Ink – The Complete Works 1968-2008
Timepieces – The Narrative Poetry
At Journey's End – The Narrative Poetry, Vol. II
The Demon Horse on the Carousel – and Other Gothic Delights
Poems of Myth & Scare – Later Narrative Poems

ISBN – 978-0-9807148-6-9

Contents

Poems written later with Chinese themes...

Foreword

In August of 2005 I was given the opportunity to travel to China to teach English for a year, at the Wenzhou Medical College, in Zhejiang Province. I was given a two bedroom apartment on the fifth floor of an eight storey apartment building in Xia Lv Pu. I caught a shuttle bus to the campus of the Wenzhou University each teaching day, at Chashan. I only worked three days a week on average, so had plenty of time to get to know Wenzhou and its people.

To say I fell in love with the place would be an understatement. For me it was a total culture clash, west to east, and it opened my eyes. These people were not the 'Yellow Peril' that I'd been taught about in my youth; they were happy, generous, resourceful and artistic, and any preconceptions I had about them fell from my eyes like scales. They made me more than welcome in their country, and I could cite many kindnesses extended to me during my stay there that convinced me they had retained something that we in the west had lost. They showed a compassion for each other, a willingness to help those worse off than themselves, and yet most lived in poor circumstances by western standards.

I was inspired to write about their culture, the good and the bad, and the result is contained in these pages. If these poems only give you a more positive feeling about China and the Chinese, I will be more than happy.

David Lewis Paget

October 2012

China

This land of ancients grows on me
Like a soft moss, damp-oozed in time,
Sad breezes churn each soul, unfree,
And sweep me over, like some tide.

Strange voices echo from dim pasts
Long littered with dead Mandarins
I hear, I understand them less
But feel their presence in old sins.

While grace and beauty walk each street
As daughters fan their coal-black hair
The future calls to them, at last
And the world waits, to meet them there.

Where Are the Birds of Wenzhou, Bei Bei

'The skies are empty and grey at dawn,
They're empty and brown at noon,
Where are the birds of Wenzhou, Bei Bei
Deep in the afternoon?
Even at dusk when the air is still
Or the cool breath heaves from the sea,
I wait for the beat of wings then, Bei Bei
Rushing to comfort me.'

'The birds were once when the paddy fields
Ran down by the river tides,
When the sky was blue and the air was clean
And the trees reached up to the stars.
The birds were here when the skies were clear
No buildings blocked the view...'
'But where are the birds of Wenzhou, Bei Bei
Why have they gone from you?'

'They left when the smog came rolling in
And the insects died on the ground,
When the grass turned white and the acid rain
Caused all the trees to drown.
They left when the river turned yellow mud
And the fields died under the road,
When men built towers of thirty floors,
They left the town in droves.'

The skies are empty and grey at dawn,
They're empty and brown at noon.

'The birds of Wenzhou took their nests
And travelled to old Hangzhou.
They went to live by a wondrous lake
That tales will tell, is blue...'
'Where are the birds of Wenzhou, Bei Bei...
Have they forsaken you?'

Black-Haired Girls

The black-haired girls are graceful, like gazelles,
Their haughty stares would strike a 'lao wai' blind,
As they cruise on through streets, where rubbish spills,
Ignoring all, the poverty, the slime.

In knee high boots and skirts that lift the thigh,
In leathers, black, and frills and pretty lace,
They swing their hips so slowly, to invite
The dreams of men, who marvel at each face.

The teeth so white and straight, the lips that curl
In condescending fashion at each gaze,
The one brow arched, as if to look on down
From some great height they fashion from each frown.

If Gods and Godesses have ever walked
This petty planet's poor and pitted earth,
Those Gods have gone, the Godesses remain,
To haunt old men, who worship at their shrine.

The Man in the Chinese Moon

Both Zhang and Tao, and Wang and Chen
They stare at the Chinese moon,
For the fifteenth day of the eighth month
They've waited and prayed at noon,
They've thought of the woman whose name is known
And written in script and rune,
They ponder her beauty and sinuous shape
As they stare at the round, full moon.

While on some hill, four girls sit still,
Their eyes raised clear to the sky,
They sigh and dream at a cold moonbeam
As they flush, turn red, and cry,
The book could tell them their future loves
But the book is held on high,
And even the children that wait to be born
Are written in ink that's dry.

The man in the Chinese Moon, Yue Lao,
Is known to them, every one,
He keeps the book under lock and key
Lists every daughter and son,
Writes every lover before they're born
Their partner, and every swoon,
Then beams and frowns as their wishes sound,
The Man in the Chinese Moon!

Blue Mountain Coffee

I take my seat at the Golden Grove
And watch the waitress, Xu,
She's sweet and pert, and her shortened skirt
Shows off a dimple or two;
She brings the menu, a pretty smile,
I get to the 'Wo xiang yao....'
But she shakes her head, before I've said
What I want, would like, or how!

She points to the meal I didn't want,
I crease my 'lao wai' brow,
'No no – Lan shan' is my one response,
'Lan shan kafei, niu nai...'
Do you have it? – this *is* a coffee shop?
All I want is a cup – that's wrong?'
She rolls her eyes, looks up to the skies
And mutters: 'Wo bu dong!'

I check my book, have I overlooked
Some word, some phrase – a tone?
'This is a 'Kafei Dian?' I say,
She brings me a chicken bone,
Immersed in water that they call soup,
I feel a sweat coming on,
I wave my hand, 'bu xing, bu xing,'
She mutters a 'Wo bu dong!'

Can you say 'Yes?' Can you say 'No?'
She shakes her head, 'Mei you!'
The sweat breaks out on my fevered brow,
'Ni ting dong ma,' I go.

She smiles so sweet, she shakes her head,
She never will understand.
'Ni lan shan kafei or not,' I cry,
She mutters 'Ni man man kan!'

'That's it, I'm off,' I shout out loud,
'Wo yiao zou le,' I roar,
She follows my every move as I
Make tracks for the outer door,
I pause and turn as I reach the street
To see her standing - then:
'Zai jian!' I snort, but she smiles at me:
'Goodbye – Please come again!'

(Glossary: - Wo xiang yao – I would like
Lan shan – Blue Mountain
Kafei – coffee
Niu nai – milk
Wo bu dong – I don't understand
Kafei Dian – Coffee Shop
bu xing – you can't/don't/ do this to me
Mei you – nothing.
Ni ting dong ma – Can you understand?
Ni man man kan – take your time.
Wo yao zou le – I want to leave. Zai jian – Goodbye).

Dragons

In the year of the Jade Emperor,
In the time of the people's pain,
The sun was hot, the people groaned
The sky gave up no rain;
'The sky gave up no rain,' he said,
'The ground was dry as a bone,
There were no rivers or lakes to feed
The crops that the people owned.
The rice lay waste in the paddy fields,
The people ate bark and clay,
While on the shores of the Eastern Sea
Four dragons laughed and played.'

These creatures, made of snake and claw,
Of horn, and fire and scale,
Looked down to see the people pray,
To hear the people wail,
So Black, and Yellow, Long and Pearl,
For these were the dragons names,
Felt sad for the people's plight, and said,
'We must bring on the rain!
Without the rain, the people die,
They are so poor and thin,
We needs must enter at Heaven's Gate
So He will intervene!'

They flew to the Jade Emperor
Who promised to send them rain,
But then sat back with his minstrel songs,
Forgot the people's pain.
For ten long days the dragons paused
To wait the darkening clouds,

14

But only saw the people cry,
Lay out their dead in shrouds.
'They laid their dead in shrouds,' he said,
'The lastborn to the first,'
The dragons said: 'He heeds us not,
Won't slake the people's thirst.'

The dragons flew to the Eastern Sea,
They knew it would bring them pain,
But to ease the hurt of the brown, dead earth
What else, but the soothing rain?
Now, dragons care for man's despair,
His hopes, his joys, his tears,
They send their many blessings down,
Relieve the people's fears.
They flew on out to the Eastern Sea
Its waters so clear and deep,
They flung it up to the heavens high
That what they'd sow, they'd reap.

Then down it came in a storm of rain
That fed the people's joy,
They laughed aloud at this water cloud
That the dragons had employed.
The moment the Jade Emperor
By the Sea God was informed,
He stamped and raged, and bellowed loud
That he would not be scorned!
He called his Generals and his troops,
To make the dragons answer,
Then called the Mountain God to him
To lie on them forever!

Caught fast beneath a mountain each
The dragons still were glad,
They'd saved the people from their pain,
The price they paid was sad;
But not unbearable, they thought,
So Long, and Black and Yellow,
With Pearl, devised another plan
That they might ever follow.
They turned their tails to rivers wide
To flow across each valley,
From West to East, the Long, the Black,
The Pearl flows, and the Yellow.

Four dragons that once cared for man,
Four dragons spread their tails,
They fed the crops that man might eat,
Might sing or dance, not wail;
The Heilongjiang is River Black,
The Dragon of the north,
And south of him, the Huanghe flows,
The Yellow Dragon's course;
The Yangtze is the Dragon Long,
The Changjiang, to the mouth,
While Pearl is now the Zhujiang,
The Dragon of the south.

Terra Cotta Warrior

You stand with all your comrades in the van,
Unflinching, you survey the sweep of time,
Your eyes are sharp and stare, the man ahead
Does likewise, and your forehead wears a frown.

In darkness you were cast, you now appear
So sudden in the light, the dawn's grey wash,
The light is harsh and bright this time of year
And soon your colours fade, then turn to ash.

But what alarm is this that breaks the spell
That Emperor Qin Shi Huang had caused to be,
Unbroken on your shoulders since he fell
And sought his bliss in heaven, on Mount Li.

What terrors brought his army to the light
Revealed the might of Qin to modern man,
The archers with their bows, when arrows sang,
The chariots and the horses in full flight.

While you, with weapon raised, prepare to march
Your armour, dirt ingrained two thousand years,
Is ready for the clash, the battle din,
The slash of sword, the whine, the thrust of spears.

So who are these, the strangers who now stare
Forever in their awe at your design?
A face familiar here, another there,
May just be from your son or daughter's line.

Be proud, Dou shi, you come at last to stand
Revealed, to prove the potter's ancient craft,
While time stands still for all who see you there
To wonder at the world, where once, he laughed.

Riding the Wenzhou Bus

They squeak and rattle, and jerk and pull
And throw you across the floor,
The double-deckers, the number 5's,
The 3's and the 64,
They come in colours of red and blue,
Of green, and in spattered mud,
They wait for no-one but bully on through,
If you get in their way - there's blood!

The seats are plastic and hard as nails,
The roof is but four feet high,
You scramble along on your knees at the back,
Unless you're a dwarf, or sly -
And climb the stairs to the upper deck
To slide in the slime, and cuss,
You need to be dressed in your army boots
When riding the Wenzhou Bus!

The brakes are shot, they rumble and howl
As they wheeze and groan to a halt,
The body sways, and the rust is foul,
And they buck like a playful colt;
The roar of the engines is petty assault,
But your ears get used to the din,
The gears grind at the stop, the start,
And as second and third slide in.

But for one and a half, or just two Kwai
You can ride 'til the day is done,
You can watch the girls in their stylish clothes
All hanging on straps, each one,

With bags and baggage and cases full,
Watch peasants, or someone's boss,
Togged out in rags or in business suits
While riding the Wenzhou Bus.

And through the murk of the window panes,
All scratched, and marked, and fogged,
The Chinese go on their friendly way,
The rest of the world unplugged,
The shops, the temples, the slums, the views
Of the parks and squares – like us!
We rattle on by for just two Kwai
When riding the Wenzhou Bus.

Swan Song

Her hair was as black as a starling's tail,
Her cheeks as pale as a swan,
Her eyes, like two slim moonstones, glowed
And her mouth was the Holy Grail.
She'd played in the dirt of the village street
So long ago, so long...
She'd swum in the pools of the mountain stream,
But now, that girl had gone.

While I still rise with the early bird
To tend to my father's fields,
As the only son of an only son
I watched the woman leave.
She cried sweet tears as she said farewell
And vowed to come back, and soon,
But the village streets of a western town
Hold nothing for Ling Xiaodan.

The weeks went by, then the months and years
And I heard of her, near and far,
She was dressed in expensive clothes, I heard,
She was driving a shiny car;
She was seen at the Beijing Opera
By a man who worked at the door,
'She glided by like a Queen,' he said,
'As her dress trailed long on the floor.'

And her wai po, down in the village square
Would brag of her daughter's girl,
'She will snare some man with a million yuan,'
She said, 'not a farmer's son.

21

Go home to your fields and forget her now,
She's not for an also-ran!'
And laughed, as the tears sprang into my eyes
For the love of Ling Xiaodan.

She came back once to the village street
To her home, as ever we must,
But carefully held her dress up high
To avoid the rubbish and dust,
I stood at the side and she looked at me,
Then turned, looked quickly away,
For Ling Xiaodan and a farmer's son
Had nothing at all to say.

But I saw her once before she left,
Alone by the mountain stream,
Her eyes were sorrowful, in remorse,
Remembering how we'd been.
'I loved you once, as a child,' she said
'But the world is harsh, and grey...
We do what our fathers want us to,
And my father sent me away.'

I sat by her then, and held her hand,
Stroking her neck, and hair,
And kissed the cheek, so pale and wan,
And I cried in a deep despair..
'You must get on with your life,' she said,
'Get a wife and a baby son;
I leave tomorrow to see the man
That my father has met in town.'

I heard that she'd wed a businessman,
And cried in the quiet gloom,

My dream had died by the mountain stream,
On that day, in the afternoon.
She worked in a shop her husband owned,
So they said, but I never heard
'Til the body was brought back home again,
That the love of my life was dead.

It seemed that she'd sold her favours there
In the rear of a grimy store,
To any man with the change to spare
While her husband played Mah Jongg.
He'd gambled his fortune, and lost it all
While his wife kept the fool from jail
With what she earned with her hands and hair,
And a mouth like the Holy Grail.

But then, a man who was ill or mad
Put his grimy hands at her throat,
And squeezed the life from the darling neck
That I'd once both loved, and stroked.
They buried her up on the mountainside
By the stream, in sight of her home,
And from where I stand in the paddy fields
I can see her pale white stone.

She'd played in the dirt of the village street
So long ago, so long...
She'd swum in the pools of the mountain stream,
But now, that girl had gone.
I married a woman I barely knew
And she bore me a black-haired girl,
With eyes like two slim moonstones, and...
A mouth like the Holy Grail.

Bibles

You brought your Bibles and printed tracts
To a land that God has no heaven in,
For Tao, Confucious and Buddha, here
Had prior claims to the hearts you'd win.

You think you're holding a secret key
To truths that nobody else has found,
But minds far greater than yours despaired,
And you just cover the same old ground.

And pride lies heavy before a fall,
And vanity masks any truths you see,
The book you cherish is short on facts,
But lives in hopes, through eternity.

While all its chapters are written in blood,
The Jews, the Arabs, the Irish fools,
The swarthy Spanish Inquisitor
Who tore the flesh that he'd save poor souls.

The Reformation of England's Church,
All done for the sake of Anne Boleyn,
While Cranmer, Lambert, and Thomas More
Paid with their lives for Henry's sin.

I have no doubt that my God is there,
And sees the world through a mist of tears,
For what we've made of his mighty plan
Should shame us all for a thousand years.

But if it's a vengeful God you seek
Who waits to punish, and bring us pain,
I know him not, for the God **I** know
Would love us all, as I love my son.

But such as you can be never told,
You're sure, so sure, and you're born again;
Be sure that you live this life, not scold,
Good works aren't done on your knees, my friend!

I Can't Find a Doll with a Chinese Face!

I've watched your children, playing in the sand,
Pretty little girls with a yellow hair-band,
Cheeky little boys with their snub-nosed faces,
Kicking and a-tripping over dragging shoe-laces,
Little brown eyes, and stubby little hands,
They laugh and delight, these children of the Han.
So why do their Ma ma's buy them little dolls
With blond hair and blue eyes from western malls?

Kan kan woman if you can can see,
Look in the mirror at your rare beauty;
Who's got the hair that would steal men's glances,
Coal black and straight, that your face enhances,
High cheek-bones, and your almond eyes
Now look at your child, be proud, be wise,
Why make them think they're less than they are
Than a blond haired bimbo in a western bar?

Sons of the dragon, and little princesses,
Need to be loved, to be held - caresses!
They should be playing with a doll just like them
Not something borrowed from a Disney production,
Toss all the Barbies and the blue-eyed babies,
Revel in the glow of your eastern features,
I'm just a westerner, wandering the place,
But I can't find a doll with a Chinese face!

The Blueshell Bar

From Monday through to Friday and,
For some, on the weekends too,
There's a constant round of students here
Attacking the Chinglish stew,
They sweat on the riddle of English tense,
Of gender, of verb and noun,
But Friday nights and their teachers here
Are ready to hit the town.

In old Wenzhou, Canadians,
The Poms and the Aussies rule,
New Zealanders with their flattened vowels,
And Yanks with their godamm drawl,
The Scots are there with the Sassenachs
Their vowels like treacle glue,
'If ye' dinna gae doun tae the Blueshell, man,
I'll nae hae a drink wi' you!'

For after a week of adjectives,
Blank faces and wo bu dongs,
They're ready to slip their traces, and
Retreat to the restaurants,
Their prepositions are shelved at last
With a proposition or two,
Then they all go down to the Blueshell Bar
Where it huddles off Wendi Lu.

From ten o'clock to the early hours
They scramble for space at the bar,
The music's played at a surly scream
Or drops to a sullen roar,

There's Chinese faces as well in there,
And girls with a shapely rear,
All perched on stools with the foreign fools
While swilling the local beer.

And down the back there's another room
Where the groups philosophise,
Over a 'Jack' or a Vodka, man,
They talk of their loves and lives,
And over the mumble of bleary talk
A voice rings out at the brink:
'The world is screwed, it's over man...
It's time for another drink!'

'It's time for another drink,' he says,
And slams a Tequila down,
A 'Jack', a Bacardi One-Five-One,
A bottle of old Tsing Dao,
'I loved her man, but I let her go...'
I hear as I hit the street,
And stagger home in the early hours...
'Are you coming back?'
'Next week!'

Pu Tong Hua

English is simple, it flitters from the tongue,
It means what it says when all's said and done,
No matter how we say it, stress it or declaim,
In English it always means the same, same, same!

Chinese is difficult, your 'Pu Tong Hua',
Is drawn in little pictures that go back so-o-o far,
And every one's a concept, with no strict meanings
Making it impossible to delve your gleanings.

As often as I study, and try as I might,
I can't get your xiang xing's or qing qing's right.
There isn't any gender; there isn't any tense,
So how can your past, present, future, make sense?

Then when I've mastered some simple Chinese
You say: 'That's fine - but it's Wenzhou-nese,
Nobody in Guangzhou, Wuhan or Beijing
Would understand a pennyworth of what you're saying!'

Every city's dialect differs from the main,
Canton-ese, Shanghai-nese, nothing is the same.
Beijing has its Mandarin, the old 'Pu Tong Hua',
But it's not what you'll hear in a Wenzhou bar.

So don't look for sympathy with adjectives and pauses,
Proper nouns or pronouns, adverbial clauses,
Your cousin's not your brother, and a 'she's' not a 'him',
But how do I tell you in your old Mandarin?

Tense!

If 'I CAN' can, it's done right away,
'I CAN' never can do it yesterday,
'I can see, I can do, I can hear, I can feel,
'I can go, I can stay, I can move, I can steal.'

If 'I COULD' ever could, then he'd do it last week
Because 'I COULD' and 'I DID' are best mates, (so to speak).
'I could see, I could do, I could hear, I could feel,
I could go, I could stay, I could move, I could steal.'

If 'I DID' ever did it, the deed has been done,
'I DID' never does it right now, old son.
'I did not - You did too - So I did, you can sue,
What I did, when I did it, I did it for you.'

If 'I WILL' or 'I WOULD' or 'I SHOULD' are your thing,
Then don't hold your breath, it'll happen next spring,
'I will go, I will come, I will be, I will see,
I would stay if I could, I should get home for tea.'

But if 'I HAVE DONE' ever comes raising his head
The time has now gone, and the battle is dead.
'I have seen, I have heard, I have said in the past
I have travelled the world, I have finished, at last.'

Lost Bloom

You are God's best-kept secret, Li Xiaojun,
Your smile lights up the dimmest, darkest day,
And in your eyes, there shines a love so strong
That men are shamed, and look the other way.

For men are shallow, falling at your feet,
Protest undying love, then look a-stare
To see some dark-eyed daughter in the street,
And think that heaven has moved, to your despair.

While you provide what life has left to give,
Though age approaches, nothing turns your head,
Your eyes are fixed on what the elders teach
That love endures, until that love is dead!

Until that love is dead, or walks away,
Your love is faithful, fixed on one alone,
But this was never seen as quite enough
By those, whose feet were always set to roam.

Your culture still dictates the way you live,
The way you cleave to thoughts he may return,
That you may once again fill up his skies,
His one horizon, once he's come back home.

In China, there's no heaven, and no hell,
Except the place the lonely woman walks,
Who, long betrayed, seeks only to dispel
Her sadness, and her dreadful sense of loss!

Forget the past, forget the wayward feet,
Look only to the future now, Xiaojun,
The best is yet to come, your lover's fate
Will seek you out, before this life has done.

Don't Let Me Die in China, Lord!

I had a fright the other night,
I dreamt that I was ill,
The Angels fluttered round my bed,
They said: 'Now you be still!'
My heart beat like a pounding drum,
The pain was like a sword,
I had one thought, and only one:
'Don't let me die in China, Lord!'

The vision would not let me be,
I saw the future clear,
The landlord breaking down the door
To find me lying there.
'The Lao Wai's gone, not paid the rent!'
He'd say in pu tong hua,
'We'd better call the embassy
They'll send around a car.'

The embassy refused the car,
They didn't want to show,
'He must belong to someone else,
He isn't ours, you know!'
The neighbours filed in through the door
To look the last on me,
And clear the flat of anything
Not quite nailed down, you see.

'He looks all right, now that he's dead,'
One mother told her son,
'Perhaps we should have talked to him,'
'- a little late now, Mum!

They say he studied pu tong hua
But never got it sussed,
We'll have to make the funeral
As if he's one of us.'

So later on that day they brought
The baskets full of flowers,
The big round silvery disks that shone
While they drew straws for hours,
For who would wail and cry for me
As I had no-one near,
So two wai po's in old black clothes
Said: 'Fifty kwai an hour!'

For fifty kwai they set their chant
And woke the neighborhood,
And no one said to keep it down,
The Chinese understood.
A funeral is a sacred thing
For Han or old Yang Wei,
They kept their vigil for three days,
Then said: 'Today's the day!'

At four o'clock that morning
In the stilly dark, forlorn,
They set up all their crackers
To erupt before the dawn,
They woke up all the neighbours
Who came down to see who wept,
While other Lao Wai's turned in bed,
Rolled over, cursed, and slept.

And then the band, it started up,
An old Han marching song,

The big bass drum beat out of time,
A little late for some;
A little early for all those
Who just had got to sleep,
I wasn't quite the flavour of
The neighborhood that week.

At six o'clock they marched away
All following the hearse,
A wooden cart pulled by four men,
I thought: 'Could things be worse?'
They marched along the highway
Disregarding life and limb,
The band it played along the way
A revolution hymn.

Then I awoke, (the pain had gone),
A-tremble, in a sweat,
I wasn't ready then, I knew,
For Buddha's belly yet!
And so I raised my eyes on high
To plead, entreat, implore:
If you would grant me just one wish:
'Don't let me die in China, Lord!'

The Crazy Lady of Jiao Ba Lu

Jiao Ba Lu is an ancient street,
The cobbles are overgrown,
A few mean dwellings still bar their doors
The others are falling down;
They say a woman who lives down there
Is three parts gone to the moon,
While children mutter a curse, or pray
When she stumbles out in the gloom.

For Gao Fang Fang has pure white hair
That blows like a ghost in the breeze,
Her eyes are wild, and she never smiles,
And she often falls to her knees;
She falls to her knees with a cry of pain
At visions *she* only sees,
And wails at night when the moon is bright,
Or shadows form through the trees.

Over the hearth of her meagre home
Is a picture of Mao Zedong,
And she is there in the picture too
A girl with an armband on,
A girl with the light of reforming zeal
That shines from her hard black eyes,
Her hair tucked under a forage cap
With the rest of 'The Helmsman's' lies.

D'eng Xiao Bei was her only love,
So young in those distant days,
But he was the son of a landlord who
Was threatened to mend his ways,

They took his land and his money too
And cast him out in the rain,
While D'eng Xiao Bei hid his head in sin,
And cried for his father's pain.

Then one dread day in the neighborhood
The Red Guards came in force,
So Gao Fang Fang put her armband on
But D'eng just hid in the house;
They dragged him out as a traitor then,
And put him up on the stage,
But D'eng Xiao Bei had nothing to say
To the Guards in their rabid rage.

They tied his arms, they made him kneel,
They beat him with sticks and a club,
'Your father, he was a landlord pig,
So you are a turtle's egg!'
They tied a sign on his chest that said:
'I love not the Chairman Mao!'
And tried to make him confess his sins;
They'd still be waiting now!

While others pelted with rocks and eggs
Fang Fang looked on with shame,
She'd loved Xiao Bei with a burning love,
But nothing was now the same,
Her comrades urged her to show her zeal
To punish the 'running dog',
So she took a breath, picked up a rock
To fling at her one true love.

The rock was sharp, bitter and hard
And tore one eye from its core,

37

D'eng stared at her with his one good eye
As his blood seeped out on the floor,
Gao Fang Fang gasped, then looked aghast
And paled at the thing she'd done,
Then watched him die as the others cried:
'Long life to Mao Zedong!'

Fang Fang went home like one deranged,
And flung the band from her wrist,
So soon, in front of the People's Court
She was termed a 'revisionist!'
For ten long years in a prison cell
She wept and cried: ' Enough!'
But the years did nothing to soothe the pain
Of killing her one true love.

And still she lives at Jiao Ba Lu,
Alone, in the dark she cries
In a part of town that's coming down,
Just like 'The Helmsman's' lies.
Those days have gone, but the lady wails
As she works away at the loom,
While the neighbours shake their heads and say:
'She's three parts gone to the moon!'

Chingl-ai

I have left my heart
In the high, high sky
That you might still see
When I'm gone, close by;
And I took your love
When you slept, sound, deep
And carried love away
Like a robber in your sleep.

I wrapped it in feathers
And put it in a sack,
Hid it in a forest, then
Carried on my back,
Took a peek at nightshine
Saw the feathers heave,
Heard a little sigh then:
'Why did you leave?'

And my tears flew wide
To the river, so long
That the banks ran over
'Til the people were gone,
I'm a one man only
Like a dark, dark star
While you sky light morning
With a face-cream jar.

I loved you then
Like I love you now
Like a heart that bursts
On an old ship's prow;

Though I had to leave
When the moon went round
I will love you forever
'Til the sun burns down.

The Endless Taxi

I staggered out of the Monkey Ba
At three... or was it four?
I'd lost my watch and wallet there,
I'd not been there before,
But after drinks or three, I think
I wasn't seeing straight,
I only knew I'd smoked my last
So knew it must be late.

I searched my pockets, plumbed the depths
And found a crumpled note,
A twenty kwai had 'scaped my eye,
Thank god for kindly fate!
I had a choice of yi bao yan,
A pack of Xinanjiang,
Or I could grab a 'jiao che' home
At a cost of shi yuan!

I chose the smokes, and spent the ten,
That left me ten to go,
I knew the cost to Xia Lv Pu
Should only be ten kwai,
I hailed a Yellow Jiao Che and
Fell in the open door,
The cabbie grunted 'na li-ah',
I mumbled: 'Xia Lv Pu!'

My eyes were somewhat fuzzy
Rolling round my empty head,
I focused on the meter box,
Its numbers glowing red,

'Shi er', it said, or twelve yuan,
That's when I sobered up;
Of course! Midnight! - the fares increase,
I didn't have enough!

We got to Xia Lv Pu too soon,
I shook my weary head,
And muttered 'Ming Hang Lu, old chum,
Qu Ming Hang Lu,' instead;
The cabbie looked me up and down,
Then shrugged and turned about,
And back we went to Ming Hang Lu,
The meter jumped about.

At fifteen kwai we hit the Lu,
I muttered, 'Qu da Xue,'
'Cos that was where the campus was,
And where I'd find old Lou;
He'd surely loan me twenty kwai
To pay for the blasted car,
But then I realised... I'd left
Old Lou at the Monkey Ba.

I tapped the dash, and said: 'Hao de!
Wo yao qu Jiang Xing Island,
The cabbie was looking murderous,
I sensed that he wasn't smiling;
They've got no sense of humour here,
They're all just money crazy,
But still he turned and gunned the cab,
The meter was looking hazy.

By thirty kwai I'd lost the plot,
The Monkey Ba had closed,

Old Lou was nowhere to be seen,
I said: 'Wo qu Hangzhou!'
He muttered something like 'Shagua!
Ni shi bendan,' he said,
I flung the Xinanjiang at him,
Jumped out the cab, and fled!

So here I am, ten miles from home,
He's headed for 'gang ting',
I think my luck is running out,
The police will run me in.
I wouldn't mind, a place to sleep
Would do me, I won't fret,
The only thing that bugs me is
I've got no cigarettes!'

(Glossary and pronunciation:
Ba – Bar. Twenty Kwai (Kwy) – 20 yuan
yi bao yan (ee bough yen) – one box cigarettes
Xinanjiang (See nan jang) – Brand of cigarettes
Jiao Che (Jou –as in ouch – Chuh) – Taxi
Shi yuan (Cher you ann) – 10 yuan).

The Beggar of Wu Ma Jie

He's laid his head on a Chinese street
There's nothing of dignity here,
He's bared his soul in a plastic bowl
For the rest of the world to jeer,
His clothes are ragged, his body is torn
With a million kinds of sin,
The sort that everyone walking past
Holds close; hides under the skin.

He lies in dirt on a filthy rag
To keep the cold from his bones,
And never utters a word to beg,
Though often he cries, or groans,
His face is one with the living earth
As he rests his head on the ground,
He's soaked by the chilling winter rains
And washed by the summer storms.

His bowl holds only a few yuan
That those with a humble heart
Might drop in shame, then hurry away
From a life that's fallen apart;
There's no compassion in passing eyes
Just the hint of a prideful sneer,
That damns us all to the final fall
As we taste of his deep despair.

Our Lord, or Buddha, in heat or cold
You lie in his wretched form,
To feel the toll of a human soul
Who's lost to his wife and home;

A man walks tall in the morning sun
Is crippled by those held dear,
Then falls to earth, is there no repair
For the beggar of Wu Ma Jie?

(Wu Ma Jie – pronounced: Oo Ma Jeer).

Dong Tou Dao

I cannot stay, I cannot go,
And where I am but you would know,
I walk where feet have walked before
But your feet linger at the shore.

The sea, immense, this great divide
With each on each, the other side,
Where once we walked as moon on moon,
Now one must light our afternoon.

That narrow beach, I see it now,
That lonely beach at Dong Tou Dao
Where you laughed once, like tinkle bells
While I went looking for strange shells.

And when you walked, so full of grace
Along the sand, that lonely place
I saw my moon reflect your eyes
With ancient wisdom, speak Chinese.

A day I will remember when
All youth has rendered folk old men,
But you will young be, fair of face
At Dong Tou Beach, I see you pace.

And all I have that keeps me sane
Are moving images – each frame
Recalls that laughing girl, that day
Repeating, like some roundelay.

My past will not now let me go
As cold and chills me overflow,
I would I had not left you now…
I left my heart at Dong Tou Dao.

China Song – (Zhōng guó gē qǔ)

Last night I heard a Chinese song
That conjured almond eyes,
It swelled and soared, and took the air
I sought to breathe, my friend,
That song poured out the sadness that
I'd seen behind your lies,
It soared and swelled, and slipped and dipped,
Heartbroken at the end.

But you just smiled and chattered,
Though your words were terse and bleak,
They hid some strange confusion, and
A hurt that would not mend,
I'd seen you cry before, with not
A tear on either cheek,
When Chinese tear-ducts dry, but cry -
It seems that you pretend.

Five thousand years of sorrow
Taught you Chinese not to weep,
To show no strong emotion, to
Accept the fate you're sent,
The pendulum that swings one way,
May cut you while you sleep,
But always swings the other way
Confucius say - my friend!

So all your love and laughter and
The sadness of your past,
Is built in to the music that your
Cultured songsters write,

And truly, when I listen
To that swelling sound at last,
Your tears well up, and overflow
From *my eyes*, every night.

Before I forget...

The China stint is over,
There's only a week to go,
I packed up a box of souvenirs
And trudged to the 'you zheng ju',
They cost me an arm and leg to send
By 'shui lu lu xin jian,'
I just have to pack a suitcase now,
Say 'ron' to a special friend.

The apartment's almost empty,
It looks quite bare, forlorn,
As bare as the heart I gave to them
The people of old Zhejiang,
Their lives will go on without me now
As I head to the 'Fei ji chang,'
But I take my memories, every one
To the land where I come from.

The children dancing at 'Dou Mei Li,'
At the end of Wendi Lu,
The neon signs, the disco bars
And the Chimp from the Wenzhou Zoo,
The rat-tat-chatter of Chinese girls
The smiles from a Chinese cop,
The crazy lady at Ming Hang Lu
At the 'I am your friend'-ly shop.

The buses rattling by non-stop
That take you to who knows where,
The moonlight rides in a trike, red top,
The crazies that drive 'Jiao Che's',

All this I'll remember while travelling home,
Then back to my life before,
But many a Chinese Moon will wane
Before I forget Zhong guo!

(Glossary and Pronunciation:
you zheng ju (Yo jung jew) – the Post Office
Shui lu lu xin jian (Shway loo loo shin jen) – Surface Mail
ron – Aussie expression – 'Catch ya late(r on).
Zhejiang (Ger –as in Germany – jang) – A Chinese Province.
Fei ji chang (Fay gee chang) – airport.
Dou mei li (Doe may lee) – Do&Me – Chicken place like KFC
Wendi Lu (Wendy Loo) – Wendi Street.
Ming Hang Lu (Meen Haang Loo) – Ming Hang Street.
'I am your friend' is the one English phrase known by this
lady.
Jiao Che (Jow – as in ouch – Tchur) – Taxi
Zhong guo (Jong gwor) – China.

Poems written since my return, with Chinese themes...

The following poems, though not written in China, have been written over the years since my return. They illustrate the hold over my mind that the Chinese experience had, and still has.

No doubt there will be more in the future...

Shoes

'Get rid of those old shoes,' she said,
'Their time has come and gone.'
I looked down at my battered soles
And smiled, as she went on;
When women talk of 'romance', then
It must be dressed to kill,
But these old shoes saw more romance
Than she could ever tell.

I took these shoes to China,
They passed through Singapore,
They trod old Wenzhou's meaner streets
In silence, pride and awe;
They padded through fine Restaurants
And stood before my class,
While Chinese students bit their pens
Translating Poe, en masse.

These shoes took me to Shanghai,
To walk the Nanjing Road,
They stood while shoppers gaily passed
And chattered some sweet code,
These shoes have trod through old Beijing
The Square, Tian'anmen,
Where Marco Polo did his thing
My shoes had followed on.

They walked the Summer Palace
Where Emperors played their roles,
A thousand years of history
Was scuffed along their soles,

They slithered over Kunming Lake
Long frozen, on the ice,
They strolled the Bronze Pavilion
Like some ancient paradise.

Then on the heights at Ba-da-ling
They helped me climb 'The Wall',
They dragged my poor old bones aloft,
I thought that I would fall,
They paced beside the Terra Cotta
Warriors at Xian,
These shoes have seen more romance
Than a new pair ever can.

'Get rid of these old shoes, my dear,
I couldn't, I regret;
I bought them when I first met you,
When we were young, my pet;
They hold too many memories
Of how we were back when;
I'll keep them underneath our bed -,'
The wife - she kissed me then!

Chinese Box

For years, the 'Muse of the Heavenly Gates'
Had stood in the shade of a country lane,
Quietly tending its residents there,
The old, the feeble, the stark insane.
The blurb said, here was a heaven on earth
For the old to pass their declining years,
It said they lived in a quiet content,
The truth was actually quite the reverse.

For Matron Margaret Parker-Lang was
A nun, expelled from the Carmelites,
'Too much of the world', they said of her,
When caught indulging in base delights.
The years had hardened, had turned her hair
An iron grey, and her eyes were cold,
She only smiled when the visitors came
To pay the fees for their aged, in gold.

She didn't encourage their visits, though:
'It's hard, you see, and they get upset,
Best to remember them how they were,
Their memories fade, then they forget.'
Few would revisit the Heavenly Gates,
They left them safe in the nurse's care,
Who drugged the residents every night
So none could complain of their treatment there.

They gathered them all in a stupor, sat
In rows, in front of a giant screen,
Then played them movies in black and white
'Til half the residents there could scream.

The food was bland and inedible,
So soon they wasted to skin and bone,
And those who thought to protest would find
They'd confiscated their telephone.

The visiting Locum, Doctor Zourk,
Had quite a collection of things antique,
Whenever he'd visit a prospect's home,
They'd be committed, within the week.
Then he and the Matron would take their pick
Of anything there that took the eye,
If anyone later complained, they'd say:
'He'd put it out for the rubbish guy!'

But once in 'The Muse of the Heavenly Gates'
The trap would spring, the shades come down,
They'd flourish the papers and help him sign
His house and his title deeds to them.
Again, when his mind was wandering
The Matron would sit, and hold his hand:
'Organ donation, that's the thing,
If you could help, that would be grand!'

I was away in China, when
My father went to the Heavenly Gates,
A note from the Matron said, 'He's fine!
Our lawyers will help him to sort his estate.'
I must have been deaf to the warning bells,
My mind was focused, I let it be,
I never once thought of the Chinese Box
That I'd taken home on a previous leave.

I'd happened on it in a Curio Shop
In the winding back streets of Xi'an,

I'd never quite managed to puzzle it out
And finally left the old box at home.
I knew it was ancient, marked and scored,
With a funny old Chinese symbol too,
The Chinese owner had bowed and smiled
When I asked what the box could really do.

It came as a shock when my father died,
We'd not been together for quite a spell,
By the time that I got back home again,
They'd taken his organs, eyes as well.
Unknown to me, he had signed a form
That I knew he'd not in the world have done,
To give them the right to his organs, once
He had passed away, and his race was run.

I was angry then, but I went on home
And braced myself for another shock,
Things were missing, a Chinese screen
And my beautiful, ancient Chinese Box.
My back was up, my suspicions rife
I sought out the Matron then, to talk,
But found her dead on the slab back there,
Dismembered by locum, Doctor Zourk.

He'd taken some of her organs out,
They sat in the open fridge nearby,
But then she coughed, and she sat up straight,
Let out a horrible, piercing cry.
The doctor staggered and ran from the room
Like a sprinter, racing right out of the blocks,
'Watch for that old antique,' she hissed,
'The dragon that came in the Chinese Box!'

She was breathing for barely a minute more
As she fell back onto the blood-soaked deck,
But what she managed to whisper there
Made the hairs rise up on the back of my neck.
She'd solved the puzzle and opened the box
When the drawer slid out with a sudden bang,
For what had jumped out and bitten her then
Was the Dragon of Emperor Qin Shi Huang.

The dragon's venom had paralyzed her,
So Zourk had thought she was good and dead,
He'd wanted the Box for himself, you see,
But she had raided our house, instead.
He thought he could sell her organs then,
And pick up the box as a plus, as well,
Collectors become more fanatical when
On that short sharp road to a personal hell!

The Box sits there by the mantelpiece
Wherever I travel, or think to roam,
I've travelled on back to China, so
The Dragon will feel that it's safe at home.
I heard that the Doctor is doing time
For the gruesome murder of Matron Lang,
Thank God - I haven't been introduced
To the Dragon of Emperor Qin Shi Huang.

The Hand of Tong Bao Lin

I stood in front of the guillotine
And paled at the sharpened blade,
The motor hummed as my mind went numb
And my body shook and swayed,
The sweat poured into my open eyes
And blinded and burned like sin,
But I had no choice, I had to be free
Of the Hand of Tong Bao Lin.

I'd worked in China for seven years
In the city of old Qingdao,
If I hadn't been such a hero, I
Would still be working there now;
But I got involved in a scuffle there
When a woman was being attacked,
He'd snatched her bag and I snatched it too,
So he turned on me, and hacked.

I'd heard of the mean Hand-Chopper Gang,
Just petty crims on the whole,
They stole whatever was not nailed down,
Just handbags, wallets and gold,
But they carried machetes under their coats
For the woman who fought like mad,
If she wouldn't let go, they'd chop off her hand
And carry it off with the bag.

I stood in shock, and stared at my wrist,
While he took off, scot free,
My hand still clutching the shoulder strap
But it wasn't attached to me,

I bled all over the pavement there,
Collapsed in a bloody heap,
I only discovered my hand was gone
When I woke from a troubled sleep.

The doctors there were marvellous,
They tidied it up no end,
But it isn't much consolation when
You can't shake hands with a friend,
I'd just about been resigned to it
When in walked Doctor Chu,
He was something to do with the government,
Said – 'I need to talk with you!'

'Let's say that it's just an experiment,
Long odds, but you may just win,
Get you a working hand again,
Though one with a yellow skin.'
I signed the form with my one good hand
And put myself in his care,
If I'd known back then what I know today...
I'd have put an axe through his hair!

They took me away that very night
To a place both dread and grim,
To one of those Chinese Prisons where
You're dead if they let you in.
They housed me there in the hospital
And treated me better than those,
The walking dead in the prison beds
Who all wore the orange clothes.

The prison was only for murderers,
And those with a capital crime,

Whose fate was lead in the back of the head
It was only a question of time.
I heard men scream as I tried to sleep,
And many a Chinese curse,
But they filled me full of some sedative,
And this only made it worse.

I dreamt as I slept there fitfully
Of a man who was chained to his bed,
As the surgeons sliced at his body there,
His screams still ring in my head;
His face contorted, he looked at me
And managed an evil grin,
As they surgically took his hand, he said:
'You be sorry... I Tong Bao Lin!'

The fever lasted for days, I think,
I thought I'd never wake up,
But then one morning my mind was clear
And my arm was bandaged up,
Slowly, slowly I felt the hand
That they'd grafted onto my wrist,
I should have been grateful then, I know,
But I slowly became obsessed.

It healed at last, took many months,
But it worked, and didn't feel strange,
I carried the hand of a dead man now
But then it began to change,
I found it reached for a woman's purse
In a shop where she'd dropped it there,
And it gripped it fast when she snatched it back,
It was more than I could bear.

I fled outside in confusion, and
Made tracks for a backstreet den,
I had no idea what drew me there
But found it was opium;
They lay around with those long, clay pipes
And the hand, it reached for one,
I knew right there I would have to share
My life with Tong Bao Lin.

The hand, it reached into pockets when
I walked on my usual beat,
It seemed attracted to shiny things
And fondled the girls on the street,
It drew me into the thickest crowds
Did things that would bring me shame,
And I'd thrust it deep in my pocket then
For the sake of my own good name.

The hand was marred by a strange tattoo
A serpent with wings, on the thumb,
When traders saw it they veered away
And one of them pulled a gun.
I stayed at home and I locked the door
And I slowly became depressed,
The hand would pound on the wall, the floor
And the lid of a rosewood chest.

A Chinese man came to call one day,
Bowed low, and I let him in,
In broken English I heard him say:
'I lookin' for Tong Bao Lin!'
He stared on down at the yellow hand,
And looked at the old tattoo,
'Bao Lin!' he pointed, 'an evil man!
You know what you have to do!'

61

And so, I stand by the guillotine,
The sweat pours into my eyes,
It takes two buttons to start the blade,
There's a demon to exorcise.
I place my wrist on the cutting line
And the man says, 'Let's begin!'
I push the button, and so does he,
The brother of Tong Bao Lin!

The House of the Scarlet Moon
(Hong Yue Liang De Fang Zi)

I fell in love with a Chinese girl
Her name was Chen Xiao Fei,
We worked together in Middle School
In the Province of Anhui,
She'd join me in my apartment when
The working day was done,
But never would take me to home to meet
Her mother, Chen Shaojun.

Xiao Fei was going on thirty, which
Had meant, in Chinese terms,
That she was a spinster, on the shelf,
She had no marriage plans,
I asked her once if she'd marry me
But she laughed and said, 'No way!
My mother would jump from the balcony
If I married an old Yang Wei.'

I called in once to the family home
To win her mother round,
She glared at me as I paced the floor,
Her father sat and frowned,
She wouldn't sit at the table while
I stayed there, under her roof,
But screeched at her daughter, in Chinese,
Some slang that was quite uncouth.

She came one day to say, Xiao Fei,
The wedding date was set,
I asked her who was the lucky man -
But she'd not even met him yet!

Her mother had schemed and arranged it all
To thwart what plans we had,
She cried a bucket of silent tears
But would do as her mother said.

She stayed away for a month or two
To let things settle down,
Then married the man that her mother chose
From a village, out of town.
When a month had passed, I was feeling lost
'Til there came a knock at my door,
It was Chen Xiao Fei in some deep dismay
So I sat with her, down on the floor.

She clung on tight to my shoulder, sobbed,
And cried, wouldn't let me go,
The man she'd married was such a brute
As the marks and the bruises showed,
But worse than that, she looked at me
As her eyes had begun to mist,
'I'm having a child, and I don't quite know
If the baby's yours, or his!'

I sat quite shocked in the evening gloom,
And I felt a sudden chill,
'You'll know as soon as the baby's born,'
I said, but my heart stood still.
If she should deliver a foreign child
She'd be left in a deep disgrace,
And her family then would turn their backs
From the horror of 'losing face'.

Our fears were proven a few months on,
The child was a baby boy,

At first the father and parents danced,
They couldn't conceal their joy,
In China, there is the one child rule,
One chance is all that you get,
So girls go missing there all the time
If the father's mind is set.

For sons are valued as girls are not,
A boy can work on the farm,
A girl will grow to be someone's wife,
Will travel away from home.
So often, just when the child is born
The father will wait outside,
The judge and the executioner,
It's often a question of pride.

A boy is swept up in loving arms,
A girl will wait on the thumb,
If the thumb goes down then the baby drowns
Or is dumped in the cinder drum.
If a boy is born with a fatal flaw,
His fate is the same as hers,
Or he may be sold to a heartless soul,
They call it the Chinese Curse!

The boy was fine 'til he opened his eyes
And they saw that his eyes were blue,
His skin was yellow, his hair was black
But the eyes... the eyes... They knew!
Not even a day had passed before
The baby had paid for our sin,
He was sold to a beggar for ten yuan,
A beggar named Sun Lang Lin.

The birth, already forgotten there
Was marked – 'delivered but dead!'
The Doctor was paid a forgetting fee,
As Xiao Fei cried in her bed,
She told me, when she returned to work,
What they'd done with our beautiful son,
She looked aside, avoided my eyes,
Pretended they'd done nothing wrong.

It took me a month to discover the name
Of the beggar, Sun Lang Lin,
I haunted the areas beggars haunt,
But could find no sign of him,
Then just by chance, a crippled child
Who begged by a streetside bin,
Cowered away when I asked her the way
To the beggar called Sun Lang Lin.

She raised a hand to protect herself
At the sound of his hated name,
She said that he'd kicked and he'd beaten her
Had crippled and brought her to shame,
This child was one of a dozen he had
Who begged for him, night to noon,
She whispered his place of ill-fame in my ear,
'The House of the Scarlet Moon'.

I couldn't find anyone willing to talk about
Where this old Tavern was,
I knew it was out in the countryside,
Beside a deserted Mosque.
I travelled by day and I slept rough at night
As I searched in the dusk and the gloom,
Then finally, there in the distance I spied
The House of the Scarlet Moon!

Sun Lang Lin lay in his dirty rags
On a bed on the floor at the back,
I waited 'til midnight, picked up a rock
And I worked out my plan of attack,
Children were crying in fitful sleep
In a room in that dark old den,
I crept through the dark to the crying there
To look for my blue-eyed son.

Around the walls were earthenware jars
And each with a child within,
He'd jammed them in tight, where nothing could grow,
Their legs would be twisted and thin,
This house of horrors and nightmares kept
Its secrets all wrapped in gloom,
My son lay there on a coverlet,
In the House of the Scarlet Moon.

I seized my son, I smashed the jars,
The children fell to the floor,
They each were maimed and deformed, I knew,
They'd never be able to walk,
They'd spend their lives in the gutters for him,
Set up with a begging bowl,
I wondered how people like Sun Lang Lin
Could open the doors to the soul.

He woke, came running right into the room,
And he pulled out a long, sharp knife,
I laid my son on the coverlet
And prepared to fight for my life,
He lunged just once, I stepped aside,
I hit him just once with the rock,

He fell and he didn't get up again
So I picked up my son, and took off.

Once well away in the undergrowth
I stopped and I turned, to see,
A flame was flickering through the roof
Of the Tavern that used to be.
It all went up with a mighty roar
As I hugged my son in the gloom,
There's no more babies, or cripples made
At the House of the Scarlet Moon!

Family History

My father left when I was one,
Or maybe two - I don't recall,
I have no memory of him now,
No memory then, now none at all.

It didn't seem important then
I had my mother, she had me,
And Uncle George would call each day,
Call by most nights, and stay for tea.

I wasn't even curious,
My world was perfect as it was,
We lived beside a village green
And travelled by the village bus.

Our house was large, a mansion set
In Parklands, much too large for us,
Whole wings were closed and boarded in,
My mother said, 'it makes less fuss!'

It wasn't 'til I went to school
That doubts arose about my kin,
The boys would taunt and tease me there,
Would comment on my yellow skin.

They called me 'Squinty' for my eyes,
They looked so different then, to them,
My hair was black and very straight:
'You'll never make an Englishman!'

I asked my mother why I looked
So different, just like chalk and cheese,

69

She smiled and held me close to her,
And said: 'Your father was Chinese!'

'I met him through your Uncle George,
They served together in some war,
He charmed me once, but then he left,
Went off to fight for Chiang-Kai-shek.'

'I thought that he'd return one day
But truth to tell, he never did,
I heard that he'd been killed before
The White Army had turned and fled.'

She mentioned words I'd never heard
'Formosa', 'Tao' and 'Mao Zedong',
'Long March', 'Red Army', words that I
Remembered when no longer young.

I grew determined then to seek
The truth behind my history,
To find my father, where he lay,
Tear back the shroud of mystery.

'Don't do it, son,' said Uncle George,
'Leave sleeping dogs to sleep the day,
For once you rouse them, sleeping dogs
Will never cease to bark and bay.'

'He's right,' my mother said, her mouth
Was set, and she looked awful grim,
'You'll bring the terrors of the night
Down on us, if you look for him!'

My mind was set, I disagreed,
With all the folly of the young,

70

I thought that I could spend my need
And so made plans to see Taiwan.

I only got as far as London,
There I went to the G.R.O.,
Asked for the Births and Deaths they kept
To settle the questions I should know.

But when the book was placed before me
Words - they swam before my eyes,
The father stated at my birth
Was George Hubertus Syndon Wise!

I faltered then, and nearly fell
My heart it plunged to the floor, and then,
The mother plainly written there
Was one they called Wang Shu Qian.

My legs were weak, I barely stood,
My father was an Englishman!
I took a breath and walked the street...
My mother, a daughter of the Han.

I went back home to the mansion then
Ignored my mother upon the stairs,
Headed right up to the West Wing floor
They had boarded and banned me from, for years.

Tore the boards from the door and entered,
Thought I would find just cobwebs there,
But saw bright lights, and heard soft music,
A woman sat in an old wing chair.

I knew, the moment those almond eyes
Met mine, I looked on my mother then,

The tears ran down from her high cheek bones
To stain her dress, Wang Shu Qian.

She'd lived forever behind these doors
All boarded in for a secret's sake,
And George had been with her, now and then
My father, living his life - a fake!

But all about there were artifacts,
Screens and parchments and vellum scripts,
Priceless furniture, paintings, figures,
Dragons, pearls, and the odd Phoenix.

George came stumbling up the stairs
His face dead white when he saw me there,
'My boy... I told you...' he said, then stopped
As grey ran worrying through his hair.

The hoard was that from a Chinese palace,
Wang Shu Qian was a keeper there,
They'd fled the rape of the communists
Taken their baggage with Chiang Kai shek.

'When things are settled we'll give it back,'
My mother told me in Pu Tong Hua,
George translated her every sentence,
Love shone out from his eyes for her.

'Her name is top of their wanted list,
They hired assassins to search for her,
We thought it best to concoct those lies
To protect you from the world out there.'

My sister took on the role of mother,
You were only a baby then,

While Shu Qian despaired to hold you,
Show you love as her only son.

The hoard has since been returned to China,
Both my mothers live openly now,
I've been taking a course in language
Coming to grips with Pu Tong Hua.

My family history seems complete,
I know as much as I need to know,
The dogs are sleeping, skeletons rest
And I won't disturb their sleep - No How!

(Note: The Chinese pronounce Chiang Kai Shek
as Jiang kuh sher.
Pu Tong Hua = Poo Tong Hwa = Beijing Dialect.
Wang Shu Qian = Wong Shoe Chee-en).

Robbing the Tomb

The year was bad, the crops were burnt,
The dragon turned his back,
The River Wei was almost dry
The earth was brown, and cracked,
The peasant army, risen up
Destroyed the House of Chin,
Set fire to all their palaces,
Their army turned and ran.

But we were left with nothing since
The death of Chin Shi Huang,
That first and greatest Emperor
Who'd ruled across the land,
He lay within his tomb up there
Hid deep within Mount Li,
And left us all with nothing but
A distant memory.

So Wang and Tong, my neighbours
With both Zheng and Shao along,
Had thought about the riches that
Lay underneath the ground,
They'd murdered all the builders and
The architects, the slaves,
So no-one could reveal the plans
Of Chin Shi Huang-ti's grave.

The ruling class were weak, had fled,
We thought this was our chance,
Why shouldn't we be rich, we thought,
We'd fought with sword and lance,

We'd long defended Chin Shi Huang
So now we should be paid,
The riches of the tomb lay there
Down where his corpse was laid.

'You know the penalty for this,'
Said Shao: 'We'll lose our heads,
If anyone should get to hear
That we've disturbed the dead.'
'We're going to die soon anyway,'
Croaked Zheng, 'you'd rather starve?
I'd risk my head for just one ring...'
The rest of us just laughed.

'What if his ghost has roamed abroad
To rage and roar at us?
Down in that ghostly sepulchre
Where he was laid in trust?'
No man survived to see beneath
Those workings that were done,
They buried all his concubines
And workmen, every one!'

'I'd face a thousand ghosts,' said Tong,
'A ghost can't do you harm,
'I hope you're sure of that,' said Wang,
Who blanched in his alarm.
'Of course they can't, we'll get to work
The moon is full tonight,
We'll tunnel down, lie low by day,
Work while the moon is bright!'

It took us just a week to find
The steps to take us in,

The air was musty, smelt of death
The death knell of the Chin.
Then Shao had lit a candle, and
Cried out, a note of fear,
We stood and stared agape at horses,
And each charioteer!

And lines of archers, infantry,
That glared us in the gloom,
A whole division of the Chin
Had filled that darkened room,
But soldiers, made of pottery,
They stood as if in death,
To wait for Chin Shi Huang to rise,
To take a mortal breath.

We made our way between the rows
An army from the past,
And every face was different there,
A grim, unsmiling mask,
There must have been a thousand, or
Ten thousand, who could tell,
The army of an Emperor
To breach the gates of hell!

Eventually we found a way
To tunnel through the walls,
Some passages led out of there
Deep down into the halls,
Where concubines were lain, asleep,
The beauties of the land,
But when Shao touched a tender cheek
The flesh was yellow sand.

So down, and deeper down we went,
The tomb must lie below,
We had no thought for safety, we
Just wandered anyhow,
And then a twang had sounded, as
A bolt took cousin Zheng,
Straight through the skull, the crossbow
That he'd tripped, was meant for him.

He died before he hit the floor,
Then other bolts flew yet,
The traps for plunderers like us
The Emperor had set,
One took Shao, entered at the throat
And pinned him to the wall,
His eyes had glazed, and then he died,
He couldn't even fall.

That left just me and Tong and Wang,
To crawl along the floor,
We came to heavy cedar doors
We knew we'd found the core,
The pictographs said 'Don't come in,
Or you will feel the curse,
Of Emperor Chin Shi Huang, your sin
Will drive your pauper's hearse!'

Tong kicked the door in with his boot,
Then ducked, and fell instead,
A blade came snaking to the floor
And Tong had lost his head!
It rolled unknowing down a stair
And landed, staring up,
From diamonds, rubies, sapphires,
And gem encrusted cups.

The coffin was magnificent,
A massive copper sheath,
And round about, such artefacts
That gleamed, beyond belief,
Wang couldn't stop, he crawled right down
And over Tong's dead form,
I screamed a warning, turned and ran,
And cursed that I'd been born!

I never saw Wang Bin again,
I made my way outside,
I slunk back home and hid for weeks,
I'd lost face, and my pride!
As Wang went down those chamber steps
I just wished that I'd hid,
For as Wang reached the jewels, I saw
The coffin raise its lid!

Dragon Lake

Bao Peng sat back and lit his pipe,
The hob was cold, the ash quite dead,
He drew a tiny firelight
That lit the scar high on his head.
While Zhang was hushed, he gathered round
Each brother, cousin; neighbours too,
'Bao Peng will not begin his tale
Until your silence begs him to!'

'In years gone by,' Bao Peng began,
'When revolution ruled this land,
Our village lived at peace back then,
We helped each other, as we can!
We grew rice in the paddy fields
Kept pigs and horses, sheep and game,
And lived, though poor, contentedly
Until the Helmsman's Red Guards came.'

'We drew our water from the lake
And shared in everything we grew,
The Buddhists had a temple there
A thousand years, for all we knew.
They held our manuscripts and deeds,
Cared for our souls, and history,
These holy men did no-one harm
But lived an ageless mystery!

The Red Guards came, in gangs and droves,
Just schoolkids really, like some mob,
With filthy mouths they screamed at us,
Then beat our women, killed our dogs.

They made us swear to love their Mao,
To hate the 'Olds' - old buildings, books,
We didn't stand a chance -' Peng stopped...
And felt the scar from Red Guard hooks!

'They killed my wife, Mei Fang,' he said,
'They stoned her up on Bullock Hill,'
The tears streamed freely down his cheeks
And we could see, he loved her still!
'And then they went down to the lake
To burn the temple, burn the books,
The monks were slaughtered, beaten down
With clubs and knives, with swords and hooks!'

'The flames came through the Temple roof,
The pages of the books were charred,
We stood well back, as well we knew
What they'd not know - the Beijing Guard!
A form stirred deep within the lake,
The waters moved, and out there slid
The monstrous shape of fang and claw,
The greatest 'Old' that ever lived!'

'The screams were heard for hours that night,
The ghastly shrieks of those devoured,
The ones who raised their clubs to me,
Dragged in the water, overpowered!
The Red Guards never came our way
Again, we held a village wake...
They should have asked, before they burned
Just why we called it - Dragon Lake!'

China Blue

I had seen him in the market,
I had glimpsed him in the rain,
I had tried to pick his trail up
On the Wenzhou-Hangzhou train,
Then he'd seen me drinking Kafei
In a little Shanghai Ba,
And had run the length of Nanjing Road
And fled in a jiao che.

He was Sun Peng Fei, her brother,
She was Sun Ye Ling, I knew,
But I'd always caught her smiling
When I called her China Blue,
She was sweet, and very pretty,
And I'd fallen for her, hard,
In the village school at Ping Yang
When I saw her in the yard.

We had taken to each other
And I'd tried to learn Chinese,
But she warned me of her brother,
He was grim, and hard to please,
And her parents had been angry
When they heard of me one day,
They had told her older brother
'She'll not marry a yang wei!'

At the end of the semester
China Blue had disappeared,
And I asked the Zhongwen lao shi
If it was as I had feared,

She'd been taken by her parents
And her brother to Shanghai,
Thinking I could never find her,
But I knew I'd have to try.

A needle in a haystack
Would be easier than this,
There are twenty million people
In this huge metropolis,
But I knew that I would see them
If I watched the Nanjing Road,
In that swarm of Christmas shoppers
I stayed put, and watched the crowd,

A week before that Christmas
I could see them, in a queue,
Lining up for western presents,
Mother, father, China Blue,
Then I tapped her on the shoulder
And she turned and smiled at me,
So I took her by the hand
And then I whispered 'Wo ai ni!'

'Wo ai ni,' she answered gladly
Flung her arms around my neck,
While the mother screeched at father,
And the father shook his head,
But they came with me together
And we sat in Mei Don Lao,
Where I slipped rings on her finger
And I made a solemn vow.

Then the mother, I won over,
And the father gave a grunt,

They agreed we should be married
If that's what we really want,
And the brother, he's no trouble
We go drinking, bowling too,
And I'm soon to be a father
With my love, my China Blue!

(Glossary:
Kafei – (Karfay) – coffee
Ba – (Bar) – Bar
Jiao che – (Jow Tcher) – Taxi
Peng Fei – (Peng Fay) – male name
Ye Ling – (Yer Ling) – female name
Yang wei – (yang way) – Foreign devil
Zhongwen Lao shi – (Jongwen Lao Sher) – Chinese teacher
Wo ai ni – (war I nee) – I love you
Mei Don Lao – (May Don Lao) – MacDonalds)

The Girl in the Mirror

I was staying in the village
That was known as Banzhushan,
In the mountains, in the Province
That the Chinese call Hunan,
It was perched atop the mountain
You could reach, and touch the sky,
But there were no single women,
And the men up there were shy.

They were poor, could offer nothing
To entice a willing bride,
They earned little from their labours,
And their houses, poor inside,
So the girls would leave to travel
Down the mountain to the plain,
Where they'd find a richer husband
Than the farmer, sowing grain.

So the men would send out raiders
To the outskirts of the towns,
And they'd kidnap straying peasants,
All the women that they found,
And they'd target younger widows
Who would not put up a fight,
Then would carry them to Banzhushan
Protected by the night.

I had met a village elder
By the name of Zhang Fan Cheng,
He was ancient, a magician,
One the Chinese call yāorén,

He invited me to dinner,
It was simple, shoots and rice,
He was dignified and courteous,
But caught me by surprise.

In the further room, a mirror
Stood at length, both straight and tall,
The frame was wrought in silver
And it leant against the wall,
He showed it to me proudly
Then asked how much would I pay?
For just 5,000 R.M.B.
He'd sell it me, today!

I reached out to feel the silver,
Was it fake or was it real?
He sensed my hesitation
Then he motioned, 'You be still!'
And plunged his hand into the glass
The mirror let him in,
His arm up to the elbow
Against science, against sin!

He reached his arm behind and pulled,
A girl came into sight,
She was standing in the mirror,
He was holding her so tight,
And she stared, while looking at me
And she said: 'Qing bang bang wo!'
I could read it on her lips, and then
The wizard let her go.

She had said: 'Would you please help me!'
But I'd stepped back in the room,

She was nowhere near behind me
Just reflected, in the gloom,
And I saw a tear forming at
The corner of her eye,
The wizard pulled his arm out, and
She waved to me, 'Goodbye!'

I paid the man his money, and
I took the mirror down
On a wooden cart he lent me,
And I took it through Hunan,
Then I packed it on a train and went
Off speeding to Nanjing,
Where I kept a small apartment,
And I turned, and locked us in.

I stood the mirror over by
A meagre wooden shelf,
Then I stood quite still before it
Hoping she would show herself,
And I tried to put my arm inside
Like he had done before,
But the mirror was unyielding,
So I stood there, and I swore!

That night the girl appeared,
Standing right behind the glass,
And she pummelled on the surface
As if she'd be free at last,
But the mirror was ungiving,
And I couldn't hear her voice,
So I took a ball pein hammer -
It had given me no choice!

She could see me through the mirror,
In alarm, she mouthed 'Meiyou!'
But her beauty had beguiled me
Though I knew she'd shouted 'No!'
I was fevered and impatient now
To set this beauty free,
So I swung the ball pein hammer
And it shattered, over me!

She fell out through the broken glass,
Lay trembling in my room,
Bleeding, sobbing in the silence,
Like the silence of the tomb,
And she said she'd been imprisoned
Since the days of Qin Shi Huang,
Then she writhed upon the carpet
As her flesh turned into sand.

I had wanted to release her
To relieve those tender tears,
But her body, once released took on
The last two thousand years;
She took one last, despairing look
Then withered up to die,
And for years I've sought the answer
To the only question - 'Why?'

The End of the Ming

Out in the hinterland the wild wolves call
While the soldiers shiver, strung along The Great Wall,
Their hands on their quivers, with their arrows, full flight
As they listen for the Manchu troops in the night.

They would beat off the peasants at the Shanhai Pass
As The Wall held firm, for the Ming's last gasp,
But the rebels beat the army of the last of the Ming,
In the city of the Emperor, the Old Beijing.

And they fired the city under Li Zicheng
While the Emperor despaired, he was called Chongzhen,
He threw a final feast for the House of the Ming,
And he called for his daughter, the Lady Chang Ping.

When the feast was over they awaited his word
But he slew each one with the point of his sword,
And his daughter too, bowed down to his will,
Then he fled the palace grounds, to Jingshan Hill.

And there with a rope on a myrtle tree
Chongzhen hung himself as high as could be,
While the leader of the peasants, this Li Zicheng,
Tried to found the Shun, as he buried Chongzhen.

But a General of the Ming, one Wu Sangui
He opened up the gates of The Wall one day,
And the Manchu troops streamed through to Beijing
Where they finished off the army, and Li Zicheng.

It was written in the stars, shining down on The Wall
That a dynasty rises as a dynasty falls,
But the soldiers on The Wall, now finished with the Ming,
Still keep a steady watch for the House of Qing.

For out in the hinterland the wild wolves call
And a soldier's duty is to guard The Great Wall,
For it little matters here about the Emperor's plan,
Just the wives and children of the soldiers of the Han!

(Glossary:
Shanhai - Shan-high,
Li Zicheng - Lee Zer Cheng,
Chongzhen - Chung Gen,
Wu Sangui - Oo Sang way
Qing - Ching)

The Ghost Brides of Shandong

When the Gao Gao clan lost its favourite son
In a coal disaster in the mines of Shandong,
He could not be buried in the family plot
For he died unmarried, with his lifeline cut.

So they wept and they wailed for a cold ghost bride
And they searched in the village and the countryside
For a girl to carry his descendant line,
But the girls were rare, and there wasn't much time.

The corpses of long dead buried are 'dry',
Taken from the grave beneath a star filled sky,
But the clan insisted on a corpse that was 'wet',
A girl too recent to be dried out yet.

89

A farmer had bought himself a girl he could sell
For a true life marriage, but the girl wasn't well,
He could get more money for a ghost, they said,
So he strangled the girl, and he sold her, dead.

The Gao Gao's bought her and dressed her in red
And they laid her beside the son that was dead,
They carried out the 'minghun' ceremony
That would bind them together for eternity.

Then they both were buried in the family plot,
And the brother gave them both a son he had got
Who carried on the line distinct for the dead.
So the dead son's spirit wouldn't rise, it's said.

In the Northern Provinces where coal holds sway
In Shaanxi, Shandong, and even Hebei,
When the miners die from a coalface fall
There are ghost brides buried who will marry them all.